This Prayer Journal Belongs To

_____

©Christian Guide Press 2019 | All Rights Reserved

How to Use this Journal

1. Pick a topic you would like to study. There are over 50 suggestions with accompanying bible verses on the next page. You are not limited to these topics, so choose another if you like.
2. Look up the suggested verse in your favorite bible translation.
3. Start your study by writing the verse in this journal (there are 50 two-page spreads to use).
4. Reflect on the verse. Underline or highlight words and phrases that you would like to learn more about.
5. Do you have any questions about the highlighted words, phases or the verse itself? If so, start digging a little deeper. There are a lot of online and offline resources to help you understand the meaning of the verse.
6. When your research is complete, reflect on the verse again. Write out the meaning of the verse, as you understand it now.
7. Now, sit back and think about how this verse applies to your life. Or, if it doesn't already, how you can apply the message.
8. Finish by writing a prayer that incorporates the meaning of this verse.

Please enjoy studying the bible with this journal.
                          Thank you and God bless you,
                          Christian Guide Press Editors

Suggested Topics & Accompanying Bible Verses

Life Matters

Anger	*James 1:19-21*
Anxiety	*1 Peter 5:7*
Caring	*Philippians 2:4*
Change	*2 Corinthians 3:18*
Depression	*Psalm 42:11*
Guilt	*1 John 1:9*
Happiness	*Matthew 5:16*
Honesty	*Proverbs 16:13*
Hope	*Romans 5:5*
Inspiration	*2 Timothy 3:16*
Justice	*Psalm 106:3*
Life	*Titus 1:2*
Loneliness	*Deuteronomy 31:6*
Loss	*Matthew 11:28-29*
Patience	*Hebrews 6:12*
Stress	*Psalm 103:1*
Temptation	*1 Corinthians 10:13*
Wisdom	*James 1:5*
Worry	*Luke 12:25*

Personal Growth

Boldness	*Proverbs 28-1*
Confidence	*Philippians 4:13*
Contentment	*Ecclesiastes 5:20*
Creativity	*Exodus 35:31*
Excellence	*2 Peter 1:3*
Health	*Proverbs 3: 7-8*
Integrity	*1 Chronicles 29:17*
Respect	*Romans 12:10*

Relationships

Children	*Proverbs 22:6*
Community	*John 13:34-345*
Courtesy	*Hebrews 13:2*
Fidelity	*Proverbs 5:15*
Friends	*John 15: 13-15*
Love	*1 Corinthians 13:13*
Parents	*Exodus 20:12*
Spouse	*Matthew 19:5*

Spiritual Growth

Blessings	*James 1:19-21*
Courage	*Ephesians 6:10*
Devotion	*Luke 16:13*
Encouragement	*Hebrews 3:13*
Eternity	*Philippians 3:20*
Faith	*Galatians 5:6*
Freedom	*2 Corinthians 3:17*
Generosity	*Deuteronomy 15:10*
Grace	*John 1:16*
Guidance	*Proverbs 1:5*
Joy	*Philippians 4:4*
Purpose	*Jeremiah 29:11*
Salvation	*Ephesians 2:8*
Serving	*1 Peter 4:10-11*
Strength	*Psalm 46:1*
Thankfulness	*Psalm 100:4*
Trust	*Psalm 118:7-8*
Understanding	*Ephesians 5:17*
Victory	*1 John 5:4*

Choose a topic and bible verse to study (use your favorite bible translation).
Or, choose your own topic and bible verse.

Lord, this is the topic I will study today

DATE: **VERSE:**

Write the Bible Verse

Question I Have About This Verse	The Answer I Found for My Question

My Interruption of this Topic

How Does this Topic/Verse Apply to Me?

My Prayer

Lord, this is the topic I will study today

DATE: **VERSE:**

Write the Bible Verse

Question I Have About This Verse

The Answer I Found for My Question

My Interruption of this Topic

How Does this Topic/Verse Apply to Me?

My Prayer

Lord, this is the topic I will study today

DATE: VERSE:

Write the Bible Verse

Question I Have About This Verse

The Answer I Found for My Question

My Interruption of this Topic

How Does this Topic/Verse Apply to Me?

My Prayer

Lord, this is the topic I will study today

DATE: **VERSE:**

Write the Bible Verse

Question I Have About This Verse

The Answer I Found for My Question

My Interruption of this Topic

How Does this Topic/Verse Apply to Me?

My Prayer

Lord, this is the topic I will study today

DATE: **VERSE:**

Write the Bible Verse

Question I Have About This Verse

The Answer I Found for My Question

My Interruption of this Topic

How Does this Topic/Verse Apply to Me?

My Prayer

Lord, this is the topic I will study today

DATE: **VERSE:**

Write the Bible Verse

Question I Have About This Verse

The Answer I Found for My Question

My Interruption of this Topic

How Does this Topic/Verse Apply to Me?

My Prayer

Lord, this is the topic I will study today

DATE: **VERSE:**

Write the Bible Verse

Question I Have About This Verse

The Answer I Found for My Question

My Interruption of this Topic

How Does this Topic/Verse Apply to Me?

My Prayer

Lord, this is the topic I will study today

DATE: **VERSE:**

Write the Bible Verse

Question I Have About This Verse	The Answer I Found for My Question

My Interruption of this Topic

How Does this Topic/Verse Apply to Me?

My Prayer

Lord, this is the topic I will study today

DATE: **VERSE:**

Write the Bible Verse

Question I Have About This Verse

The Answer I Found for My Question

My Interruption of this Topic

How Does this Topic/Verse Apply to Me?

My Prayer

Lord, this is the topic I will study today

DATE: **VERSE:**

Write the Bible Verse

Question I Have About This Verse

The Answer I Found for My Question

My Interruption of this Topic

How Does this Topic/Verse Apply to Me?

My Prayer

Lord, this is the topic I will study today

DATE: **VERSE:**

Write the Bible Verse

Question I Have About This Verse	The Answer I Found for My Question

My Interruption of this Topic

How Does this Topic/Verse Apply to Me?

My Prayer

Lord, this is the topic I will study today

DATE: VERSE:

Write the Bible Verse

Question I Have About This Verse

The Answer I Found for My Question

My Interruption of this Topic

How Does this Topic/Verse Apply to Me?

My Prayer

Lord, this is the topic I will study today

DATE: **VERSE:**

Write the Bible Verse

Question I Have About This Verse	The Answer I Found for My Question

My Interruption of this Topic

How Does this Topic/Verse Apply to Me?

My Prayer

Lord, this is the topic I will study today

DATE: **VERSE:**

Write the Bible Verse

Question I Have About This Verse	The Answer I Found for My Question

My Interruption of this Topic

How Does this Topic/Verse Apply to Me?

My Prayer

Lord, this is the topic I will study today

DATE: **VERSE:**

Write the Bible Verse

Question I Have About This Verse

The Answer I Found for My Question

My Interruption of this Topic

How Does this Topic/Verse Apply to Me?

My Prayer

Lord, this is the topic I will study today

DATE: **VERSE:**

Write the Bible Verse

Question I Have About This Verse

The Answer I Found for My Question

My Interruption of this Topic

How Does this Topic/Verse Apply to Me?

My Prayer

Lord, this is the topic I will study today

DATE: **VERSE:**

Write the Bible Verse

Question I Have About This Verse

The Answer I Found for My Question

My Interruption of this Topic

How Does this Topic/Verse Apply to Me?

My Prayer

Lord, this is the topic I will study today

DATE: VERSE:

Write the Bible Verse

Question I Have About This Verse

The Answer I Found for My Question

My Interruption of this Topic

How Does this Topic/Verse Apply to Me?

My Prayer

Lord, this is the topic I will study today

DATE: **VERSE:**

Write the Bible Verse

Question I Have About This Verse

The Answer I Found for My Question

My Interruption of this Topic

How Does this Topic/Verse Apply to Me?

My Prayer

Lord, this is the topic I will study today

DATE: **VERSE:**

Write the Bible Verse

Question I Have About This Verse	The Answer I Found for My Question

My Interruption of this Topic

How Does this Topic/Verse Apply to Me?

My Prayer

Lord, this is the topic I will study today

DATE: VERSE:

Write the Bible Verse

Question I Have About This Verse

The Answer I Found for My Question

My Interruption of this Topic

How Does this Topic/Verse Apply to Me?

My Prayer

Lord, this is the topic I will study today

DATE: **VERSE:**

Write the Bible Verse

Question I Have About This Verse

The Answer I Found for My Question

My Interruption of this Topic

How Does this Topic/Verse Apply to Me?

My Prayer

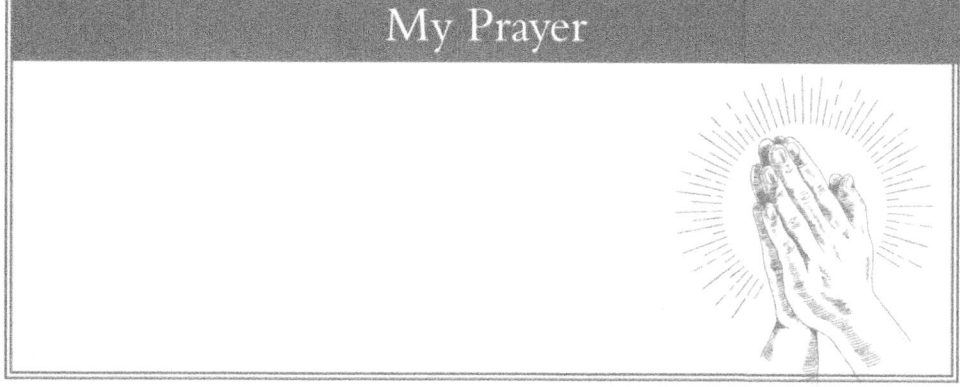

Lord, this is the topic I will study today

DATE: VERSE:

Write the Bible Verse

Question I Have About This Verse

The Answer I Found for My Question

My Interruption of this Topic

How Does this Topic/Verse Apply to Me?

My Prayer

Lord, this is the topic I will study today

DATE: **VERSE:**

Write the Bible Verse

Question I Have About This Verse

The Answer I Found for My Question

My Interruption of this Topic

How Does this Topic/Verse Apply to Me?

My Prayer

Lord, this is the topic I will study today

DATE: **VERSE:**

Write the Bible Verse

Question I Have About This Verse

The Answer I Found for My Question

My Interruption of this Topic

How Does this Topic/Verse Apply to Me?

My Prayer

Lord, this is the topic I will study today

DATE: VERSE:

Write the Bible Verse

Question I Have About This Verse	The Answer I Found for My Question

My Interruption of this Topic

How Does this Topic/Verse Apply to Me?

My Prayer

Lord, this is the topic I will study today

DATE: **VERSE:**

Write the Bible Verse

Question I Have About This Verse

The Answer I Found for My Question

My Interruption of this Topic

How Does this Topic/Verse Apply to Me?

My Prayer

Lord, this is the topic I will study today

DATE: **VERSE:**

Write the Bible Verse

Question I Have About This Verse

The Answer I Found for My Question

My Interruption of this Topic

How Does this Topic/Verse Apply to Me?

My Prayer

Lord, this is the topic I will study today

DATE: **VERSE:**

Write the Bible Verse

Question I Have About This Verse

The Answer I Found for My Question

My Interruption of this Topic

How Does this Topic/Verse Apply to Me?

My Prayer

Lord, this is the topic I will study today

_____

DATE: **VERSE:**

Write the Bible Verse

Question I Have About This Verse

The Answer I Found for My Question

My Interruption of this Topic

How Does this Topic/Verse Apply to Me?

My Prayer

Lord, this is the topic I will study today

DATE: **VERSE:**

Write the Bible Verse

Question I Have About This Verse

The Answer I Found for My Question

My Interruption of this Topic

How Does this Topic/Verse Apply to Me?

My Prayer

Lord, this is the topic I will study today

DATE: **VERSE:**

Write the Bible Verse

Question I Have About This Verse

The Answer I Found for My Question

My Interruption of this Topic

How Does this Topic/Verse Apply to Me?

My Prayer

Lord, this is the topic I will study today

DATE: **VERSE:**

Write the Bible Verse

Question I Have About This Verse

The Answer I Found for My Question

My Interruption of this Topic

How Does this Topic/Verse Apply to Me?

My Prayer

Lord, this is the topic I will study today

DATE: VERSE:

Write the Bible Verse

Question I Have About This Verse

The Answer I Found for My Question

My Interruption of this Topic

How Does this Topic/Verse Apply to Me?

My Prayer

Lord, this is the topic I will study today

DATE: **VERSE:**

Write the Bible Verse

Question I Have About This Verse

The Answer I Found for My Question

My Interruption of this Topic

How Does this Topic/Verse Apply to Me?

My Prayer

Lord, this is the topic I will study today

DATE: **VERSE:**

Write the Bible Verse

Question I Have About This Verse	The Answer I Found for My Question

My Interruption of this Topic

How Does this Topic/Verse Apply to Me?

My Prayer

Lord, this is the topic I will study today

DATE: VERSE:

Write the Bible Verse

Question I Have About This Verse

The Answer I Found for My Question

My Interruption of this Topic

How Does this Topic/Verse Apply to Me?

My Prayer

Lord, this is the topic I will study today

DATE: **VERSE:**

Write the Bible Verse

Question I Have About This Verse

The Answer I Found for My Question

My Interruption of this Topic

How Does this Topic/Verse Apply to Me?

My Prayer

Lord, this is the topic I will study today

DATE: **VERSE:**

Write the Bible Verse

Question I Have About This Verse

The Answer I Found for My Question

My Interruption of this Topic

How Does this Topic/Verse Apply to Me?

My Prayer

Lord, this is the topic I will study today

DATE: **VERSE:**

Write the Bible Verse

Question I Have About This Verse	The Answer I Found for My Question

My Interruption of this Topic

How Does this Topic/Verse Apply to Me?

My Prayer

Lord, this is the topic I will study today

DATE: VERSE:

Write the Bible Verse

Question I Have About This Verse	The Answer I Found for My Question

My Interruption of this Topic

How Does this Topic/Verse Apply to Me?

My Prayer

Lord, this is the topic I will study today

DATE: **VERSE:**

Write the Bible Verse

Question I Have About This Verse

The Answer I Found for My Question

My Interruption of this Topic

How Does this Topic/Verse Apply to Me?

My Prayer

Lord, this is the topic I will study today

DATE: VERSE:

Write the Bible Verse

Question I Have About This Verse

The Answer I Found for My Question

My Interruption of this Topic

How Does this Topic/Verse Apply to Me?

My Prayer

Lord, this is the topic I will study today

DATE: **VERSE:**

Write the Bible Verse

Question I Have About This Verse

The Answer I Found for My Question

My Interruption of this Topic

How Does this Topic/Verse Apply to Me?

My Prayer

Lord, this is the topic I will study today

DATE: **VERSE:**

Write the Bible Verse

Question I Have About This Verse	The Answer I Found for My Question

My Interruption of this Topic

How Does this Topic/Verse Apply to Me?

My Prayer

Lord, this is the topic I will study today

DATE: **VERSE:**

Write the Bible Verse

Question I Have About This Verse	The Answer I Found for My Question

My Interruption of this Topic

How Does this Topic/Verse Apply to Me?

My Prayer

Lord, this is the topic I will study today

DATE: **VERSE:**

Write the Bible Verse

Question I Have About This Verse	The Answer I Found for My Question

My Interruption of this Topic

How Does this Topic/Verse Apply to Me?

My Prayer

Lord, this is the topic I will study today

DATE: **VERSE:**

Write the Bible Verse

Question I Have About This Verse	The Answer I Found for My Question

My Interruption of this Topic

How Does this Topic/Verse Apply to Me?

My Prayer

Lord, this is the topic I will study today

DATE: **VERSE:**

Write the Bible Verse

Question I Have About This Verse

The Answer I Found for My Question

My Interruption of this Topic

How Does this Topic/Verse Apply to Me?

My Prayer

Lord, this is the topic I will study today

DATE: **VERSE:**

Write the Bible Verse

Question I Have About This Verse

The Answer I Found for My Question

My Interruption of this Topic

How Does this Topic/Verse Apply to Me?

My Prayer

Made in the USA
Monee, IL
14 March 2022